Usborne Spotter's Guides

Country Walks

Edited by Karen Goaman and Phillip Clarke

Consultants: Peter Holden,
Geoff Howe, Dr Margaret Rostron,
Dr Mark Spencer

Usborne Quicklinks

The Usborne Quicklinks Website is packed with thousands of links to all the best websites on the internet. The websites include information, video clips, sounds, games and animations that support and enhance the information in Usborne internet-linked books.

To visit the recommended websites for Spotter's Country Walks, go to the Usborne Quicklinks Website at **www.usborne-quicklinks.com** and enter the keywords: **spotters country**

Internet safety

When using the internet please follow the internet safety guidelines displayed on the Usborne Quicklinks Website. The recommended websites in Usborne Quicklinks are regularly reviewed and updated, but Usborne Publishing Ltd is not responsible for the content or availability of any website other than its own. We recommend that children are supervised while using the internet.

Usborne Publishing is not responsible and does not accept liability for the availability or content of any website other than its own, or for any exposure to harmful, offensive, or inaccurate material which may appear on the Web. Usborne Publishing will have no liability for any damage or loss caused by viruses that may be downloaded as a result of browsing the sites it recommends.

Contents

How to use this book

This book will help you to identify some of the common animals and plants you may see on a country walk in the British Isles, or parts of Europe.

Identification

Each different type of plant or animal is called a species. All the species in this book have a picture and a description to help you identify them. The example below shows you how the descriptions work:

Scorecard

On page 60 is a scorecard, which gives you an idea of how common each species is. A common type scores 5 points, and a rarer one is worth 20. If you like, you can tot up your score after a day's spotting.

Useful words

If there are any words you don't understand, look at the list of useful words on pages 58–59.

➡ **Heath speedwell** —— Species name and description

A low, creeping plant which forms large mats. Found in grassy places, —— Where to find it woods, and on heaths. 30cm. May–August

| |
Average size   When it
or size range   flowers

Small circle for you to tick when you've seen a species.

Some entries have close-up views to aid identification

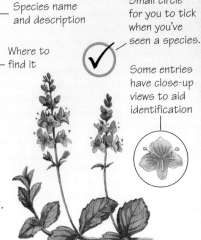

Sex symbols

Some male and female animals look very different. In this case, both sexes are shown, marked by these symbols:

 ♀ Female   ♂ Male

Picture (not to scale)

4

Measurements

The plants and animals in this book are not drawn to scale, but the average size of each species is in its description. The measurements are in millimetres (mm), centimetres (cm) or metres (m) and the pictures below show you how they are measured.

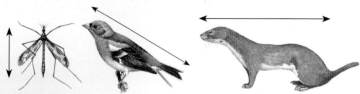

Birds, reptiles, amphibians, spiders and most insects are measured by total length, including tail, but not legs, feelers or antennae.

Most mammals are measured by body length (BL), which excludes the tail.

Snails are measured along the shell.

Butterflies, moths and dragonflies are measured by their wingspan (WS).

Hoofed mammals are measured to their shoulder height (SH).

Plants, including trees, flowers and grasses, are measured by height.

Trees are shown as they look in summer. Deciduous trees also have a small silhouette of their winter outline.

Fungi are measured by width (across the cap for mushrooms and toadstools).

Looking at the countryside

The natural home of a living thing, the area that contains all it needs to survive, is called its habitat. While you are out spotting, looking at the types of countryside habitats around you will give you an idea of the species you are more likely to spot.

Hedgerows

Marking the boundaries between fields and running alongside roads, hedgerows are an important habitat for butterflies, birds and small mammals. They often act as natural corridors between woodlands, too.

Woodland

Broadleaved woodlands are often light, open, and rich in wildlife. Conifer plantations tend to be dark, with fewer plants and animals.

Heathland

Heathland is a wide open lowland habitat with sandy soil. Plants include heather, gorse and bracken. Similar landscapes in uplands are called moorland.

Grassland

Rolling downs, old meadows and commons, and even churchyards, can provide a grassland habitat where flowers and insects flourish.

Grasslands like these are home to many other living things besides sheep.

The countryside code

• **Be safe – plan ahead and follow any signs**. Check a weather forecast before you leave, taking heed of any warnings. Ensure that your maps are up to date. Make sure somebody knows where you're going, and when you should return, and that you are familiar with the way markers that show accepted paths.

• **Leave gates and property as you find them**. Farmers may leave gates shut to stop animals escaping, or open to allow them to reach food and water. When walking through crop fields, keep to the edges, or use clearly marked paths, to avoid damaging the plants.

• **Protect plants and animals, and take your litter home.** Litter is not just ugly, it can harm animals that try to eat it. Don't start fires: one stray match can cause massive damage to wildlife or property.

• **Keep dogs under close control.** Dogs must always be kept on a lead on farmland. In the UK, farmers are allowed to shoot any dog that worries their animals.

• **Consider other people**. When riding a bike, slow down for horses and other animals, so as not to scare them. Leave farmers who are moving herds plenty of room.

Seasonal sights

Spring

In spring, in deciduous woods, leaves have just begun to grow, so light can filter through the branches, letting flowers bloom. Look out for tree blossoms, too.

You can listen for birds singing as they try to attract a mate. Later in the season, you may see them carrying twigs and other materials to build nests.

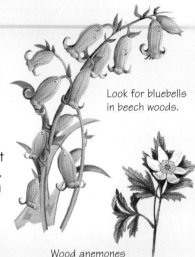

Look for bluebells in beech woods.

Wood anemones grow in oak woods.

Jay carrying twigs to nest

Beech blossom

Silver birch catkins

Perched amongst tree blossom, this yellowhammer sings to woo a mate.

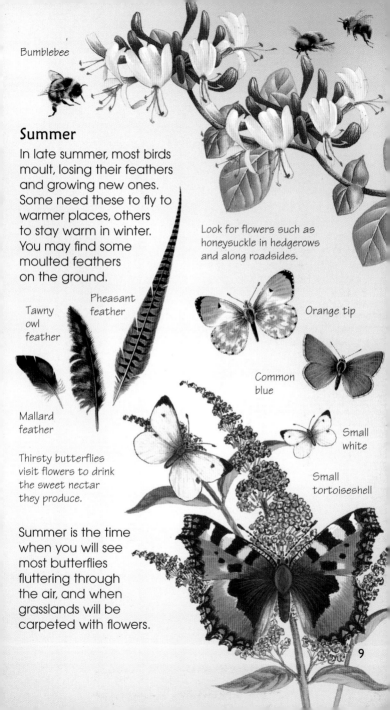

Bumblebee

Summer

In late summer, most birds moult, losing their feathers and growing new ones. Some need these to fly to warmer places, others to stay warm in winter. You may find some moulted feathers on the ground.

Look for flowers such as honeysuckle in hedgerows and along roadsides.

Tawny owl feather

Pheasant feather

Orange tip

Common blue

Mallard feather

Thirsty butterflies visit flowers to drink the sweet nectar they produce.

Small white

Small tortoiseshell

Summer is the time when you will see most butterflies fluttering through the air, and when grasslands will be carpeted with flowers.

9

Autumn

When autumn arrives, most berries and fruit are ripe, and the leaves of deciduous trees start changing colour. You'll notice an array of shades, from bright yellow and orange to dark copper and bronze.

Also look out for flocks of birds gathering in trees and on overhead wires before they migrate to warmer countries.

Swallows migrate south before winter.

Maple

Horse chestnut

Rowan

Beechnut

Beech

Brambles provide birds with shelter and berries.

This is the best time of year to spot fungi, as they flourish in the damp, mild weather, often appearing overnight, as if by magic.

Amethyst deceiver

Hedgehogs look for worms and insects to eat before going into hibernation.

Winter

While most plants die down in winter, evergreens such as holly are still flourishing, and late fruits can be seen on other plants.

Pine trees remain green over winter and you might spot cones on their branches.

Old man's beard is named after its downy winter fruits.

With many trees leafless, it's a good time to look at winter buds. These protect the infant leaves until they burst into life in spring.

Many animals hibernate in winter, resting in cosy burrows through the cold months. Others, such as squirrels, can be seen out and about, looking for food they stashed in autumn.

Grey squirrel

Beech

Ash

Sweet chestnut

Sycamore

Swan, ducks

➡ Mute swan

Seen all year on rivers
and lakes. Normally
silent, but if irritated
hisses or gives a
snorting grunt.
Young are called
cygnets. 152cm

Long neck helps it
feed under water

Cygnets

♀

♂

⬅ Mallard

Found on many
ponds, lakes and
rivers. Wild mallards
often cross-breed
with domestic farm
ducks. Only the
duck (female) goes
"quack". 58cm

➡ Tufted duck

Seen on ponds,
lakes and reservoirs.
More common in
winter. Dives for food
and can swim under
water. The drake (male)
has a long tuft. The
female's is shorter. 43cm

♀

Tuft

♂

Heron, rails, gull

➡ Grey heron

Usually seen near fresh water and estuaries. Feeds, often from the water, on fish, frogs and small mammals. Nests in trees. 92cm

Black crest

Long legs which trail out in flight

⬅ Coot

Usually seen on lakes and reservoirs, sometimes near towns. Adult birds have a white "shield" on forehead. Dives to feed on water plants. 38cm

➡ Moorhen

Lives near water, including small ponds. Prefers places surrounded by thick vegetation. Feeds on land and in water. 33cm

Red bill with yellow tip

Summer

Winter

⬅ Black-headed gull

Common inland and near the sea. Has dark brown head in summer only. In winter, head turns white with brown smudge. 38cm

Kestrel, pheasant, lapwing

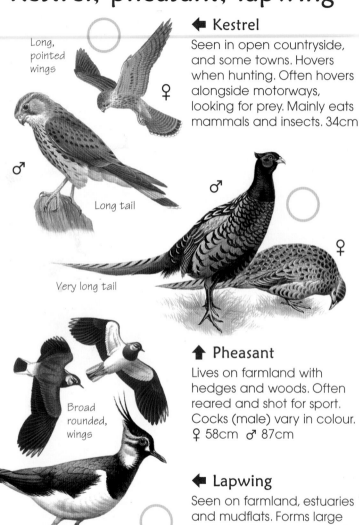

Long, pointed wings

♀

♂

Long tail

Very long tail

Broad rounded, wings

← Kestrel

Seen in open countryside, and some towns. Hovers when hunting. Often hovers alongside motorways, looking for prey. Mainly eats mammals and insects. 34cm

↑ Pheasant

Lives on farmland with hedges and woods. Often reared and shot for sport. Cocks (male) vary in colour.
♀ 58cm ♂ 87cm

← Lapwing

Seen on farmland, estuaries and mudflats. Forms large flocks in winter. Looks black and white at a distance. Its call is "pee-wit". 30cm

Pigeon, dove, woodpecker, wagtail

➡ **Woodpigeon**

A common bird of farmland, woods and towns. Forms large flocks in winter. Its call is a familiar "coo-coo-coo, coo-oo". 41cm

White on wings

White on tail

⬅ **Collared dove**

Often found around farm buildings, and in gardens and parks. Feeds mainly on grain. Often perches on wires or roofs. 30cm

➡ **Great spotted woodpecker**

Lives in woods, nesting in tree holes. Drums on trees with beak in spring. Has a bouncing flight. 23cm

♀ ♂
Large white patches on wings

➡ **Pied wagtail**

Seen mainly on farmland and near fresh water. Also found in towns. Tends to run rather than walk. 18cm

Tail bobs constantly

Swift, swallow, dunnock, wren

➡ Swift

A summer visitor, found in Britain from May to August. Flocks fly rapidly over towns and countryside. Listen for its screaming call. 17cm

Forked tail

Underside all dark apart from whitish throat

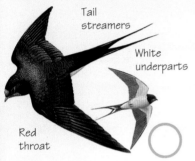

Tail streamers

White underparts

Red throat

⬅ Swallow

Summer visitor to Britain, found April to October. Often seen near fresh water. Catches insects in flight. Nests in buildings. 19cm

➡ Dunnock

Lives in bushy places such as woods, parks and gardens. Looks a bit like a female house sparrow (see opposite page), but with a grey head and thinner beak. 14cm

Shuffles along the ground

Often cocks its tail up

Very small bird

⬅ Wren

Found in all kinds of places, including woods, heaths, parks and gardens. Loud song finishes with a trill. Never keeps still for long. 9.5cm

Sparrow, robin, starling, blackbird

← House sparrow

Very common. Lives near houses and even in city centres. Often seen in flocks. Has a chirping song. 15cm

→ Robin

A woodland bird, also common in parks and gardens. Has a warbling song and a "tic-tic" call when alarmed. Male and female look alike. 14cm

Red face and breast

← Starling

Very common. Found on farmland, in woody places, parks and towns. Often roosts in huge flocks. Mimics songs of other birds. 22cm

→ Blackbird

Lives where there are trees and bushes, often in parks and gardens. Male has a lovely, loud fluting song. 25cm

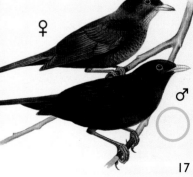

Thrush, tits

➡ Song thrush

Often seen in gardens, in or near trees and bushes. Breaks open snail shells by smashing them against a stone. 23cm

Speckled breast

⬅ Coal tit

Most common in pine woods, but also seen in broadleaved trees, and gardens. White patch on back of head. 11cm

Black band on belly

➡ Great tit

The largest tit. Lives in woodlands, heaths and gardens. Nests in holes in trees. Note its black and white head. 14cm

May hang upside down when feeding

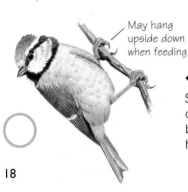

⬅ Blue tit

Seen in woods, hedgerows and gardens. Look for the bright blue on top of its head. 11cm

Finches

← Bullfinch

Often found on the edges of woods, in hedges and in gardens. Eats seeds. Its white rump shows in flight. 15cm

➡ Chaffinch

Likely to be found wherever there are trees and bushes, including gardens. Often flocks with other finches in winter. 15cm

← Goldfinch

Feeds on the seeds of thistles and other weeds in open places. Look for its red face and yellow on wings. 12cm

➡ Greenfinch

A yellowish-green bird seen on woodland edges. Also on farmland and in gardens, especially in winter. 12cm

Crows

➡ Rook

Nests in large groups in treetop "rookeries". Is usually seen in flocks on farmland. Call is a harsh "caw". 46cm

Young lack bare skin around beak

Baggy thigh feathers

⬅ Magpie

Seen amongst trees, on farmland and in towns. Eats eggs and young of other birds in spring. 46cm

➡ Jay

A secretive bird of woody areas and large gardens. It often hides in trees, but listen out for its screeching call. 32cm

⬅ Carrion crow

Common bird with a strong, curved beak, found in all types of country. Often feeds on carrion (dead and decaying animals). Has a rather heavy flight. 47cm

Fox, squirrel, rabbit, hedgehog

➡ Red fox

Lives on farmland and in woods, but also common in towns and cities. Feeds mainly at night, catching small mammals, wild birds and chickens. BL 65cm

Bushy tail

⬅ Grey squirrel

Common in woods, parks and gardens. Its coat may have patches of brown. Red squirrels are much rarer and live mainly in northern woods. BL 27cm

➡ Rabbit

Common on farmland and hillsides. Large groups live together in underground burrows called warrens. Feeds on plants. Active dusk and dawn. BL 40cm

Prickles

⬅ Hedgehog

Seen in hedgerows, woods, ditches, parks and gardens. Active mainly at night. Snuffles, squeals and snores. Rolls into a ball when alarmed. BL 25cm

Deer, shrew, vole, mouse

➡ Fallow deer

Lives in herds in parks and woods. Only buck (male) has antlers, and loses these after the mating season (the "rut") in October. SH 1m

White spots ♂

Black nose

♂

➡ Roe deer

Lives in woods, near water. Red-brown in summer, grey-brown in winter. As with fallow deer, only buck has antlers, lost after summer rut. Barks when alarmed. SH 70cm

Long snout

⬅ Common shrew

Seen in woods, hedgerows, dunes and marshes. Has a very shrill squeak. BL 7cm

Small ears

Furrier than a mouse

Short tail

➡ Field vole

Quite common on open ground. Rarely climbs, but makes tunnels through long grass. BL 11cm

Big ears

Tail as long as body

⬅ Wood mouse

Found in hedgerows, woods and gardens. Digs burrows. Climbs and moves quickly, making long leaps. BL 9cm

Stoat, weasel, snake, frog, toad

➡ Stoat

Found in many habitats. Northern stoats turn white in winter and are called ermines. BL 25cm

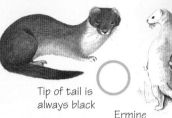

Tip of tail is always black

Ermine

Short tail

⬅ Weasel

Smaller than a stoat, and found mostly on lower ground. BL 20cm

➡ Grass snake

Harmless snake found in grassy places. Can stay under water for an hour. 70cm

Yellow and black "collar"

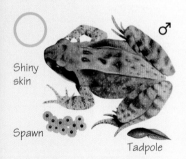

♂

Shiny skin

Spawn

Tadpole

⬅ Common frog

Found in wet, shady places. Mates and lays eggs ("spawn") in water, from which tadpoles hatch, and grow into adult frogs. 8cm

➡ Common toad

Can swim, but goes into the water only to breed. Tadpoles develop in the same way as frogs.
♀ 8.5cm ♂ 5.5cm

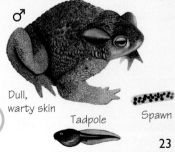

♂

Dull, warty skin

Tadpole

Spawn

23

Butterflies

♂

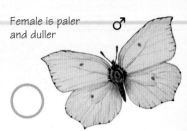

← Brimstone

Seen in hedges and along woodland paths. Caterpillar feeds on buckthorn bushes.
WS 59mm

➡ Small tortoiseshell

Visits all kinds of flowers. Quite common all over Britain. Seen from April to November.
WS 50mm

➡ Meadow brown

Seen in meadows and grassy places where it visits thistles, knapweed, and bramble flowers.
WS 50–55mm

♂　　　　♀

➡ Small heath

Found in all kinds of countryside – open woods, marshes and dry hillsides. Likes hawkweed flowers.
WS 34mm

➤ Common blue

Size and markings vary. Found almost everywhere but prefers downs and rough meadows. WS 28–36mm

Bird's-foot trefoil

♀

Caterpillar

♀

♂

♂

◄ Painted lady

Arrives in spring from North Africa. Lays eggs on thistles. WS 64mm

➤ Red admiral

Common in grassy places and gardens. Migrates from North Africa. Spiky greenish to black caterpillar makes a "tent" out of the nettles it eats. WS 67mm.

Butterflies

➡ Peacock

Common in open fields, woodland and gardens. The caterpillar feeds on nettles. Butterflies seen April to September. WS 65mm

The markings are like "eyes" on a peacock's tail

Cabbage leaf

♂

♀

➡ Large white

Found in woods, open country and gardens. Caterpillar eats cabbage plants. Butterflies seen from April to October. WS 63mm

♀

Moths, bee, wasp

⬅ Garden tiger moth

The larva is more often seen than the adult moth. Found near vegetation in all kinds of places including paths and gardens. WS 65mm

Larva is called a "woolly bear"

➡ Six-spot burnet moth

This moth, and the similar five-spot burnet, fly by day over grassy areas. WS 35mm

Larva on vetch. Other food plants are clover and bird's-foot trefoil.

⬅ Buff-tailed bumblebee

These big, common bees are seen near flowers from spring to late summer. Worker 11–16mm. Queen 17–22mm.

Pale tail end

➡ Common wasp

Attracted to fruit and other sweet things, but feeds mainly on insects. Seen mostly in late summer. 11–20mm long

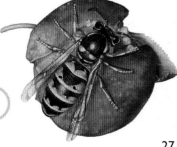

Damselfly, dragonfly, beetles, ant

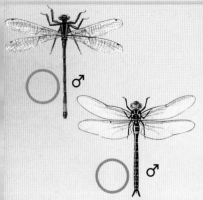

← Blue-tailed damselfly
Seen on plants near still or slow-moving water in summer. WS 35mm, 30mm long

← Common hawker
This dragonfly breeds around bogs and moors. It may be seen hunting insects near woodlands in the evening. WS 95mm, 74mm long

➡ Seven-spot ladybird
As common as the two-spot ladybird. Both are found in all kinds of places with vegetation. 5–8mm

← Violet ground beetle
Common in woods, under hedges and in gardens. Eats other insects, and worms. 25mm

➡ Red ant
This common, stinging ant nests under stones or in rotting wood. Like all ants, males and queens grow wings and mate in the air. 3–6mm

Nest in tree stump

Cricket, earwig, cranefly, spider, snail

← Speckled bush cricket

Seen in late summer or early autumn in shrubby places. Bush crickets have antennae longer than their bodies. 10–20mm

➡ Common earwig

Eats small, usually dead, insects, as well as leaves and fruit. Males have curved pincers; females' are straighter. 15mm

♂

← Giant cranefly or daddy-longlegs

Often near water or in gardens. Larvae (called "leatherjackets") eat root crops and grass roots. 30–40mm

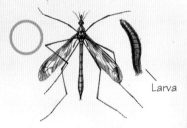

Larva

➡ Garden spider

Spins a web to catch flies and other insects. Female is much larger than male. Not an insect but an "arachnid", having eight legs. 7–18mm

← Garden snail

Common mollusc. Found on long grass, or old walls. Hides under stones in daytime, feeds on plants at night. Shell 25–35mm

Yellow flowers

← Ragwort

Tallish plant with flat-topped flowerhead. Grows in all kinds of dry, grassy places. 30–150cm. June–Oct

Very shiny leaves and flowers

→ Lesser celandine

A small, creeping plant with glossy, heart-shaped leaves and shiny flowers. In damp, shady woods and along waysides. 7cm. Feb–Apr

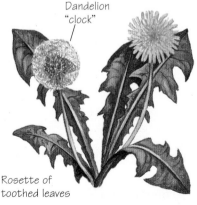

Dandelion "clock"

Rosette of toothed leaves

← Dandelion

Common plant of waysides. The flowers close at night. Look for the "clock" of downy white fruits. 15cm. Mar–Oct

◀ Primrose

Early spring flower with a rosette of hairy leaves. Often grows in patches in woods, hedges and fields. 15cm. Feb–May

➡ Creeping buttercup

Common in damp, sometimes bare, grassy places. Look for the long creeping stems ("runners") near the ground. 50cm. May–Aug

Slightly hairy stems and leaves

Cluster of fruits with hooks

◀ Herb Bennet or wood avens

Look in woods, hedges and shady places. Fruits have hooks which catch on animal fur or clothing. Up to 50cm. June–Aug

➡ Gorse

Dark green, spiny bush. Grows on heaths and commons. The flowers smell like coconut. 1–2m. Flowers all year.

Close-up of flower

31

Yellow flowers

The clustered seed pods look like birds' claws

◀ **Bird's-foot trefoil**

Look for this small creeping plant in grassy places and on downs. Also called "bacon and eggs" because flowers are streaked with red. 10cm. May–July

Bract

➡ Groundsel

Common in fields and other cultivated places. Green bracts make flowers look unopened. 8–45cm. Flowers all year.

◀ Honeysuckle

Climbing plant seen in hedges and woods. Has very fragrant flowers. Fruits are poisonous berries which ripen to red in autumn. Up to 6m. June–Sept

32

Pink flowers

➡ Cuckooflower

Grows in damp places such as
meadows, and on roadsides
especially near streams.
Flowers can be pink, lilac
or white. 15–60cm. Apr–June

⬇ Herb Robert

Spreading plant which grows
in woods, hedgebanks, and
walls. Leaves may go red in
autumn. 40cm. Mar–May

Close-up of fruit

Fluffy white
seeds seen
in autumn

➡ Rosebay willowherb

Tall plant with spikes of pink
flowers. Common on edges
of woods, roadsides,
and waste ground.
30–120cm. July–Sept

Pink flowers

➡ Wood sorrel

A creeping woodland plant with slender stems and rounded leaves. Grows in woods, hedges and shady places. 10cm. Mar–Apr

White flowers tinged pink by purplish veins

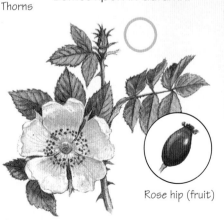

Ripe berry (edible)

⬅ Blackberry or bramble

Dense woody plant that climbs up hedges. Grows in woods, along paths and lanes, and on waste ground. Up to 3m. June–Sept. Berries ripen in autumn.

Thorns

➡ Dog rose

Scrambling shrub up to 3m tall, with thorny stems. In autumn, look for the red fruits, called rose hips. Hedges and woods. June–July

Rose hip (fruit)

Fruit

◀ Red campion

Grows in woods, hedges and other shady places. Has a hairy stem. Flowers are deep to pale pink. 60cm. May–June

➡ Large bindweed

Look for the large, pink or white funnel-shaped flowers. Climbs walls and hedges on roadsides, in waste places and along railways. Climbs up to 3m. July–Sept

Flower bud

Arrow-shaped leaves

◀ Ragged Robin

Flowers have ragged pink petals. Found in damp meadows, marshes and woods. 30–70cm. Apr–June

35

Pink and red flowers

➡ Heather or ling

Often covers very large
areas of heath and moor.
A low-growing, shrubby
plant with spikes of pink
or, rarely, white flowers.
20cm. July–Sept

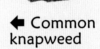

Close-up
of flower

Black bracts

⬅ Common knapweed

Found in grassland, by
roads and hedgerows.
Brush-like, dark pink
flowerheads. 40cm.
June–Sept

Long spike of
tube-shaped
flowers

➡ Foxglove

Grows in woods, hedgerows
and other open places.
Very poisonous. Has
large, oval leaves.
Up to 1.5m. June–Sept

➡ Scarlet pimpernel

Grows along the ground, on farmland and roadsides. The flowers close in mid-afternoon and in bad weather. 15cm. June–Aug

Flowers may also be blue

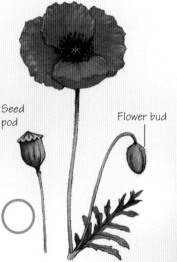

Seed pod

Flower bud

⬅ Poppy

Grows on waste ground, roadsides and cornfields. The soft, red flowers have dark centres. Stiff hairs on stem. Up to 60cm. June–Aug

Close-up of flower

➡ Wood woundwort

Strongly smelling plant of hedges, woods and other shady places. The leaves were once used to dress wounds. 40cm. June–Aug

Blue and purple flowers

➤ Bluebell

Forms thick carpets in
woods in spring. Has narrow,
shiny leaves and clusters
of nodding blue flowers.
30cm. Mar–May

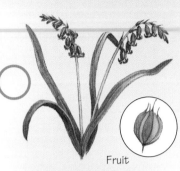

Fruit

◄ Field scabious

Grows on roadsides, dry
grassland, and in hedgerows.
To 80cm. June–Oct

◄ Devil's bit scabious

Found in marshes, damp
woods, meadows and
roadsides. To 75cm.
June–Oct

Tendril

Lobed
leaves

Field scabious   Devil's bit scabious

➤ Tufted vetch

Scrambling plant with
clinging tendrils. Climbs
up hedgerows, alongside
paths and lanes. Has
brown seed pods in
late summer. Up to
200cm. June–Aug

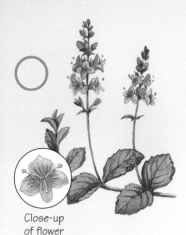

◀ Heath speedwell

A low, creeping plant which forms large mats. Found in grassy places, woods, and on heaths. 30cm. May–Aug

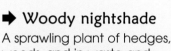

Close-up of flower

➡ Woody nightshade

A sprawling plant of hedges, woods, and in waste and damp places. The stems grow up to 2m long. Poisonous berries turn from green to red. May–Sept

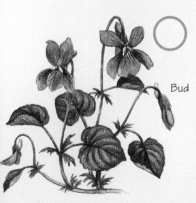

Bud

◀ Common dog violet

Low-growing plant of woods and hedges. May grow in clumps. Heart-shaped leaves. 10–20cm. Mar–May

White flowers

Split petals

← Greater stitchwort

Look in woods and hedgerows for this slender, creeping plant. Has grass-like leaves. 16–60cm. Mar–June

➡ Cow parsley

Found on hedgebanks, paths, roadside and by ditches. Also called Lady's lace. Up to 1m. May–June

Close-up of flower

Fruit

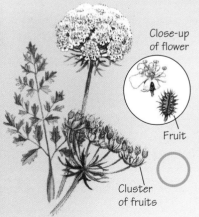

Close-up of flower

Fruit

Cluster of fruits

← Wild carrot

Grows in grassy places, often near the coast. There are many white "umbellifers" which, like this plant and cow parsley, have umbrella-like clusters of white flowers. 60cm. July–Aug

← Ox-eye daisy

Grows on roadsides and grassy places. Up to 60cm. June–Aug

Fruit

→ Goosegrass or common cleavers

Scrambling plant of hedgerows. The prickly stems stick to clothes and fur. Up to 60cm. June–Sept

Flowers grow in rings around stem

← White dead-nettle

Called a dead-nettle because, unlike common nettles, its hairs do not sting. Grows in hedgerows and waste places. Up to 60cm. May–Dec

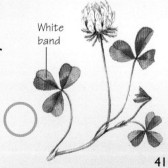

White band

→ White or Dutch clover

Creeping plant found in grassland, waste places and in gardens. Often grown for animal feed. 10–25cm. Apr–Aug

41

White and green flowers

➤ Jack-by-the-hedge or garlic mustard

Grows in hedges and open woods. Smells of garlic. Up to 1.2m. Mar–May

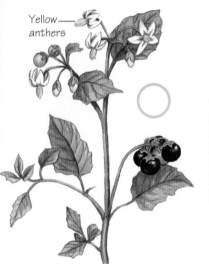

Yellow anthers

◀ Black nightshade

Bushy, low-growing plant of cultivated ground. Petals fold back to show yellow anthers. Poisonous berries turn from green to black. 20cm. July–Sept

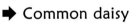

➤ Common daisy

Grows in short grass and is found in most garden lawns. The flowers close at night and in bad weather. Up to 10cm. Mar–Oct

Fruits

← Old man's beard or traveller's joy

Clambers over hedges and up trees. Look out for it in winter, when its grey, downy fruits look like a beard. Up to 30m. July–Sept

➡ Greater plantain

Found on all kinds of cultivated land, paths, waste places and on garden lawns. 15cm. May–Sept

Anthers are mauve at first, changing to yellow

Adult leaf has smooth edge

Young leaf is lobed

← Ivy

Evergreen woody plant. Climbs up trees, fences and walls. Glossy leaves often have pale veins. Has black berries in winter. Sept–Nov

43

Fern and fungi

← Bracken

A common fern often covering large areas of heaths and open woods. The broad, leaf-like "fronds" turn rust-brown in autumn. 1–2m

→ Turkeytail

A "bracket" fungus which grows from trees and stumps. 2–5cm wide. Seen all year.

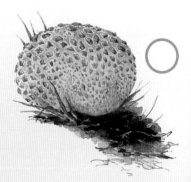

← Shaggy ink cap

Often found in groups on roadside verges and in fields. Slender, hollow stem. Cap 5–10cm across. May–Nov

→ Common earthball

Round-bodied fungus with a warty, brownish-yellow surface, and no stalk. Found in woods. Poisonous. 4–8cm across. July–Dec.

WARNING
Never eat wild fungi
without expert advice,
as many are poisonous
varieties, or are easily
confused with them.

Mature
stage with
orangey-
red cap

Young stage
with bright
red cap

➡ Fly agaric

Grows under birch and
pine trees, often on
shady soil. Poisonous.
Cap 6–12cm. Aug–Nov

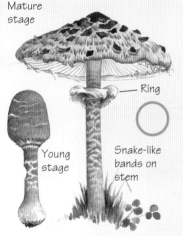

Mature
stage

Ring

Young
stage

Snake-like
bands on
stem

⬅ Parasol

Found in woods and
grassy places. Stem has
snake-like patterns and
is swollen at base. Cap
5–15cm. July–Nov

Yellowish-green
underneath cap

➡ Sulphur tuft

Grows in large clusters
on broadleaved tree
stumps. Faint ring on
stem. Poisonous. Cap
4–10cm. Aug–Nov

Broadleaved trees

Tree in flower

↟ Common hawthorn

A small, thorny tree or shrub. Has clusters of small white flowers in May. The berries are called haws. Common in thickets and hedgerows. 8m

Dark red berries

Tree in flower

↟ Elder

A common shrub of roadsides. Has creamy white flower clusters from June to July. Berries ripen from green to black in September. 9m

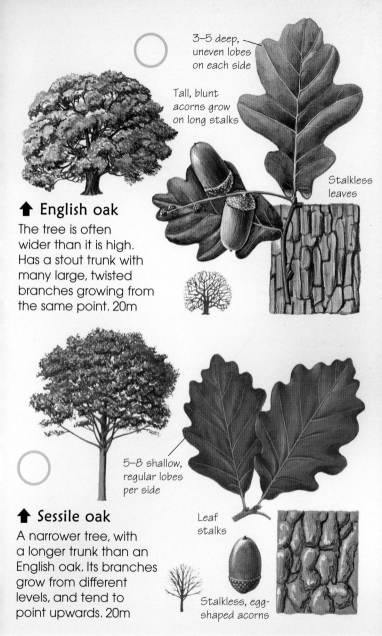

3–5 deep, uneven lobes on each side

Tall, blunt acorns grow on long stalks

Stalkless leaves

⬆ English oak

The tree is often wider than it is high. Has a stout trunk with many large, twisted branches growing from the same point. 20m

5–8 shallow, regular lobes per side

Leaf stalks

⬆ Sessile oak

A narrower tree, with a longer trunk than an English oak. Its branches grow from different levels, and tend to point upwards. 20m

Stalkless, egg-shaped acorns

Broadleaved trees

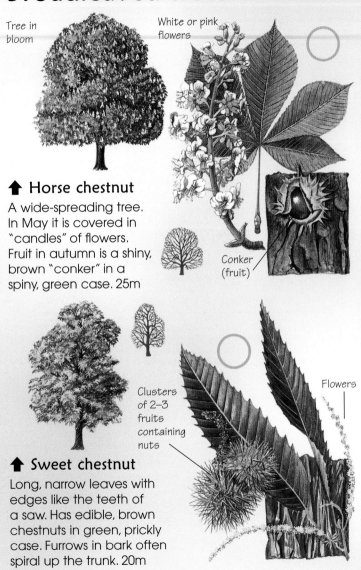

Tree in bloom

White or pink flowers

⬆ Horse chestnut

A wide-spreading tree. In May it is covered in "candles" of flowers. Fruit in autumn is a shiny, brown "conker" in a spiny, green case. 25m

Conker (fruit)

Clusters of 2–3 fruits containing nuts

Flowers

⬆ Sweet chestnut

Long, narrow leaves with edges like the teeth of a saw. Has edible, brown chestnuts in green, prickly case. Furrows in bark often spiral up the trunk. 20m

Oval leaves with crinkly edges

↑ Common beech

Wide-spreading tree. Its light green leaves turn copper-brown in autumn, and cover the forest floor all winter. Triangular nuts in prickly husk. Smooth, grey bark. 25m

Nuts in husk

9–13 "leaflets" on each leaf stalk

Winged fruits

↑ Common ash

Flowers before it grows leaves. Has winged fruits called keys which can be seen on trees throughout winter. Its branches curve up at their tips. 25m

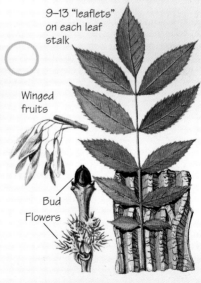

Bud

Flowers

Broadleaved trees

Pale underside of leaf

Long, narrow leaves

Catkin

↑ White willow

Like most willows, leaves are much paler underneath. Common by streams and rivers, and in wet woods and marshes. Catkins show in April. 15m

Pointed leaf-tips

Catkin

Silvery bark peels off in ribbons

↑ Silver birch

Grows in woods and on heathland. A slender tree with branches drooping at the tips. The catkins or "lamb's tails" appear in April. 15m

↑ Sycamore

A large, spreading tree often seen on roadsides and in woods. Brownish-grey scaly bark has orange patches. Fruit is a pair of winged seeds. 20m

Winged seeds twist as they fall

Berries appear only on female trees

↑ Holly

Leathery evergreen leaves are bright and shiny, with thorny prickles. Small white flowers in summer, followed by red berries. Can be a small tree or shrub. 10m

Two kinds of flower

Broadleaved trees

Close-up of a flower

Leaves turn red in autumn

↑ Rowan

Grows in woods, on mountains and along roadsides. Has clusters of creamy-white flowers in May. The red berries ripen in August. 6m

Leaf shape varies

↑ Lombardy poplar

Tall, narrow tree often planted along roadsides. The branches grow upwards from near the ground. Has pointed, triangular leaves. 28m

Furrowed bark

Conifers

Cone has 3-pointed bracts

⬆ Douglas fir

A tall conifer, seen in forestry plantations and large gardens. The lowest branches often bend down almost to the ground. Light brown, hanging cones. 40m

Bracts

Long, bare trunk red near treetop

Short, paired needles

⬆ Scots pine

Seen in woods on sandy soils and in plantations. Has bluish-green needles in pairs. Pointed cone. Mature trees have a long, bare trunk with red bark near top. 20m

Bark flakes off in places

Grasses

➡ Timothy grass

Flowerheads usually green. Pastures, roadsides and wasteland. Used to make hay for animals. 40–150cm

➡ Red fescue

Very common in old pastures, lawns and salt marshes. Has very fine leaves. 20–90cm

Flowers can be green, purplish or reddish

Timothy grass   Red fescue

⬅ Common couch grass

Common on farmland and wasteland. Rough, dark, grey-green leaves. 30–120cm

⬅ Soft rush

Common rush growing in clumps in damp or marshy places. Rounded, tube-like, dark green leaves. Green-brown flowers. 30–150cm

Common couch grass

Soft rush

White, pale green, pink or purplish flowers

➡ Yorkshire fog

Seen in meadows, pastures, lawns and saltmarshes. Soft, velvety, grey-green leaves and purple seed-heads. 20–100cm

Crops

➜ Wheat

Europe's biggest crop. Mainly used for making bread flour and animal feed. Up to 100cm

➜ Barley

Grown mainly for animal feed. Some used in beer-making. Up to 100cm

Seed-heads of grain crops are only seen in summer

Long spikes, called awns

Close-up of grain

Close-up of grain

Wheat ⬭

Barley ⬭

⬅ Oats

Will grow on fairly poor soil, without much sunshine. Mostly grown in northern Britain. Used mainly as animal feed; some used for porridge. Up to 120cm

Close-up of grain

➜ Oil-seed rape

Grown for the oil in its seeds. Leftovers used as winter feed for cattle. Turns the fields bright yellow when it flowers in late spring. Up to 160cm

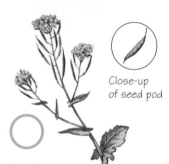

Close-up of seed pod

⬅ Sugar beet

Sugar is extracted from the white root, and the leafy tops are fed to animals. Provides about half of Britain's sugar. Up to 100cm

55

Cattle

➡ British Limousin

These ginger to red cattle are the most common breed in the UK. They are bred mainly for beef. SH 1.4m

Bull

Cow

⬅ Holstein Friesian

These large, black and white cows produce more milk than any other breed. SH 1.52m

➡ Charolais

Originally from France, this heavyweight, creamy-white breed is mainly farmed for beef. SH 1.5m

Bull

Bull

⬅ Aberdeen Angus

This hardy, black Scottish breed has no horns. It is esteemed for the high quality of its meat. SH 1.4m

Sheep and pigs

➡ Scottish blackface

A tough sheep that lives on hills and moors. The most common breed in Britain. Both rams (males) and ewes (females) have horns. SH 70cm

Ram

Ewe

Mottled face

⬅ North of England mule

This widespread sheep is a cross between a long-woolled Bluefaced Leicester and a hill breed, such as a Swaledale. SH 70cm

➡ Suffolk

A hornless breed with a black head and legs, and short, white wool. Renowned as sires (fathers) of high-quality lambs. SH 77cm

No horns

Ram

Upright ears

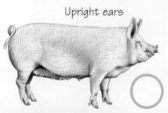

⬅ Large white

This big, common, pale pink pig is bred mainly for bacon. Can have more than 14 piglets in a litter. SH 91cm

➡ Gloucester Old Spot

The ancestors of this spotty pig used to live in orchards, eating windfall apples. Usually kept outdoors, Old Spots are prized for their tasty pork. SH 89cm

Lop ears

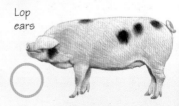

Useful words

These pages explain some words you might come across when reading about flowers, trees and animals. Words that are written in *italic text* are explained in their own entries.

amphibian – A type of soft-skinned animal that lives both on land and in water, such as a frog or toad

antenna (plural: **antennae**) – one of a pair of feelers on an *insect*'s head used for feeling and smelling

anther – part of a flower that releases *pollen*

arachnid – a type of small creature with no backbone, a segmented body with a tough covering, and eight legs

blossom – flowers, especially those on a tree

bract – a leaf-like structure at the base of a flower or stalk, or at the base of a *cone* scale

broadleaf – a tree that has wide, flat leaves. Most broadleaved trees are *deciduous*

bud – an undeveloped shoot, leaf or flower

cap – the top part of a *fungus*

catkin – an often sausage-shaped cluster of tiny flowers, all of the same sex, growing on one stalk

clearing – an area of land that has few or no trees, in the middle of a wooded area

colony – a group of the same *species* that live together

cones – the fruits of *conifers*

conifer – a tree with needle-like or scaly leaves, which bears *cones*, with their seeds inside. Most are *evergreen*.

creeping plant – a plant that grows low along the ground

deciduous – losing its leaves over a few weeks, usually in autumn

estuary – a place where a large river meets the sea. Fresh water mixes with sea water, and at low tide there are large areas of mud.

evergreen – losing its leaves gradually, throughout the year, so the plant is always green

food plant – a plant that an *insect species* feeds upon

frond – the leaf-like part of a fern

fruit – a plant's seed-bearing part

fungus – (plural: **fungi**) a type of living thing, such as a mushroom or toadstool, that can't make food from sunlight and carbon dioxide, as plants do, but feeds on plant or animal matter

habitat – the area where a plant or animal *species* lives, and which provides it with all it needs in order to survive

hibernation – a state of rest in which some animals spend winter

insect – a type of small creature with no backbone, a segmented body with a tough covering, and six legs. Most have wings.

larva – (plural: **larvae**) the young stage of an *insect*, which looks very different from the adult. For example, a caterpillar is the larva of a butterfly.

lowland – a low-lying, fairly flat region

mammal – a type of animal with a backbone, usually four limbs, and hair, that feeds its young with milk

migration – a regular movement of animals from one place to another and back again. Many birds, for example, breed in one country, then migrate to another for the winter. Migrating birds are called migrants or visitors.

mollusc – a type of soft-bodied animal, often with a protective shell, such as a snail

moult – when animals replace their fur or feathers

pasture – fields of grass grown for farm animals to eat

plantation – an area of plants or trees planted deliberately

pollen – a powder that is passed from male to female parts of flowers, enabling seeds to form

predator – an animal that hunts and eats other animals

prey – an animal that is hunted and eaten by other animals

queen – a large, breeding female in a group of *social insects*, such as ants

rails – a group of birds that includes moorhens and coots

roost – (1) when a bird sleeps (2) a place where birds sleep

rump – an animal's rear end, above its tail

rut – the mating period of deer and other hoofed animals

saltmarsh – a marshy area that is regularly flooded with sea water

social insects – *insects*, such as ants or some types of bee, that live in a *colony*, often controlled by a *queen*

species – a group of plants or animals that all look alike, behave in the same way and can breed together. For example, jays are a bird species.

sepal – a leaf- or petal-like growth which protects a flower bud, and supports the flower when it opens

shrub – a woody plant with several stems that tends to grow to less than 6m (20ft) high

upland – an area of relatively high ground

visitor – *see* **migration**

worker – a small working female in a group of *social insects*

Scorecard

When you start spotting, you'll soon find that some plants and animals are rarer than others. To give you a rough idea of how likely you are to see them, all the flowers, trees, birds, mammals and insects in the book are listed here with a score next to each one. Common species score 5 points; rarer ones are worth 20. If you want to, you can use the "Date spotted" boxes to record when you saw each species.

Species	Score	Date spotted	Species	Score	Date spotted
Aberdeen Angus	10		Collared dove	5	
Barley	5		Common ash	5	
Bird's-foot trefoil	10		Common beech	5	
Black nightshade	10		Common blue	5	
Blackberry	5		Common couch grass	5	
Blackbird	5		Common daisy	5	
Black-headed gull	5		Common dog violet	10	
Blue tit	5		Common earthball	10	
Bluebell	10		Common earwig	5	
Blue-tailed damselfly	5		Common elder	5	
Bracken	5		Common frog	5	
Brimstone	10		Common hawthorn	5	
British Limousin	5		Common shrew	10	
Buff-tailed bumblebee	5		Common toad	10	
Bullfinch	15		Common wasp	5	
Carrion crow	5		Coot	5	
Chaffinch	5		Cow parsley	5	
Charolais	10		Creeping buttercup	5	
Coal tit	10		Dandelion	5	

Devil's bit scabious	10		Herb Bennet	10
Dog rose	15		Herb Robert	10
Douglas fir	10		Holly	5
Dunnock	5		Holstein Friesian	5
English oak	5		Honeysuckle	5
Fallow deer	20		Horse chestnut	5
Field scabious	10		House sparrow	5
Field vole	15		Ivy	5
Fly agaric	15		Jack-by-the-hedge	5
Foxglove	10		Jay	10
Garden snail	5		Kestrel	10
Garden spider	5		Knapweed	10
Garden tiger moth	10		Lady's smock	10
Giant cranefly	5		Lapwing	15
Gloucester Old Spot	10		Large bindweed	10
Goldfinch	10		Large white (butterfly)	5
Goosegrass	5		Large white (pig)	5
Gorse	10		Lesser celandine	5
Grass snake	15		Lombardy poplar	10
Great spotted woodpecker	10		Magpie	5
Great tit	5		Mallard	5
Greater plantain	5		Meadow brown	5
Greater stitchwort	5		Moorhen	5
Greenfinch	20		Mute swan	5
Grey heron	10		North of England mule	5
Grey squirrel	5		Oats	10
Groundsel	5		Oil-seed rape	5
Heath speedwell	10		Old man's beard	10
Heather	5		Ox-eye daisy	10
Hedgehog	15		Painted lady	10

Parasol	10		Song thrush	10	
Peacock (butterfly)	10		Speckled bush cricket	10	
Pheasant	5		Starling	5	
Pied wagtail	10		Stoat	20	
Poppy	10		Suffolk (sheep)	10	
Primrose	10		Sugar beet	5	
Rabbit	10		Sulphur tuft	10	
Ragged Robin	15		Swallow	10	
Ragwort	5		Sweet chestnut	10	
Red admiral	10		Swift	10	
Red ant	10		Sycamore	5	
Red campion	10		Timothy grass	5	
Red fescue	5		Tufted duck	10	
Red fox	10		Tufted vetch	10	
Robin	5		Turkeytail	5	
Roe deer	20		Violet ground beetle	5	
Rook	10		Weasel	20	
Rosebay willowherb	5		Wheat	5	
Rowan	5		White clover	5	
Scarlet pimpernel	10		White dead-nettle	5	
Scots pine	5		White willow	5	
Scottish blackface	5		Wild carrot	10	
Sessile oak	10		Wood mouse	15	
Seven-spot ladybird	5		Wood sorrel	5	
Shaggy ink cap	5		Wood woundwort	10	
Silver birch	5		Woodpigeon	5	
Six-spot burnet moth	15		Woody nightshade	10	
Small heath	5		Wren	5	
Small tortoiseshell	5		Yorkshire fog	10	
Soft rush	5				

Index

Designed by Ruth Russell and Joanne Kirkby
Digital manipulation by Keith Furnival and Mike Olley
With thanks to Sarah Khan and Naomi Hopkins

Illustrated by Joyce Bee, Trevor Boyer, Hilary Burn, Victoria Goaman,
Ian Jackson, Annabel Milne, Chris Shields, Peter Stebbing and Phil Weare

PHOTO CREDITS: Cover (top) © Peter Titmuss/Alamy;
Cover (bottom) © Elizabeth Whiting & Associates/Alamy;
2–3 © David Williams/Alamy; 6–7 © The Irish Image Collection/Corbis;
8 © David Tipling/The Image Bank/Getty Images; 11 © Peter Arnold, Inc./Alamy

This edition first published in 2009 by Usborne Publishing Ltd.
Usborne House, 83–85 Saffron Hill, London, EC1N 8RT, England.
Copyright © 2009, 1982 Usborne Publishing Ltd. The name Usborne
and the devices ♀ ♀ are Trade Marks of Usborne Publishing Ltd.

Printed in China